Marian Valley

STATIONS OF THE CROSS

Nihil Obstat: Australia, 29 September 2022, Fr. Albert Wieslaw Wasniowski OSPPE

Imprimatur: Australia, 27 October 2022, ✠Columba Macbeth-Green OSPPE

The stations of the cross used in this book are adapted from those found in *Modlitwy Zakonu Świętego Pawła Pierwszego Pustelnika, Częstochowa - Jasna Góra 2015* which was published in English as *Order of St. Paul the First Hermit Prayer Book, Australia 2018*. They remain the property of the Order St. Paul the First Hermit and may not be used without permission.

The Stabat Mater is the translation by Edward Caswall, *Lyra Catholica* (1849). Bible quotes are taken from the *RSV CE*.

Editor: Fr. Joseph Maria Buckley OSPPE
Published by: The Pauline Fathers and Brothers Australia
2541 Beechmont Rd, Witheren, Qld 4275
paulinefathers.org.au or marianvalley.org.au
Publication ©The Pauline Fathers and Brothers Australia 2022
ISBN: 978-0-6456438-2-4

Stations of the Cross

It is the practice where possible to start the stations of the cross kneeling before the altar where an act of contrition is made, and the intention is formed of gaining the indulgences connected to the devotion, whether for themselves or the souls in Purgatory. They say:

Preparatory Prayer

My saviour, you made this journey, this way of the cross, out of love for me while I was still a sinner and unworthy of your love. As I recall this journey, may I remember the grace that I received at baptism and be filled with a desire to be ever more faithful to it, knowing that so many times in my life, I have not repaid you with gratitude for what you did for love of me.

They cried out, "Away with him, away with him, crucify him!" ... Then Pilate handed him over to them to be crucified.

John 19:15-16

First Station

Jesus is condemned to Death

℣. We adore Thee, O Christ, and we praise Thee,

℟. Because by Thy holy cross Thou hast redeemed the world.

Leader: Every path to holiness begins here, with the first station of the Cross. The decision to put the will of God first. Remember that fully aware of what would happen, Christ accepted being scourged and crowned with thorns and though innocent to be condemned to death. Choose also to enter this road, this pilgrimage of the cross.

People: O most holy Will of God, may I seek only you and may the fulfilment of your Will be my greatest delight. Lord Jesus, may you be for my soul as a true vine is to its branches.

Our Father... Hail Mary... Glory Be...

℣. Lord Jesus, crucified,

℟. Have mercy on us!

> At the Cross, her station keeping,
> Stood the mournful Mother weeping,
> Close to Jesus to the last.

So they took Jesus, and he went out, bearing his own cross, to the place called the place of a skull, which is called in Hebrew Gol gotha.

John 19:17

Second Station

Jesus is made to carry His Cross

℣. We adore Thee, O Christ, and we praise Thee,

℟. Because by Thy holy cross Thou hast redeemed the world.

Leader: Jesus began the road of his suffering in the Garden of Gethsemane. Later that night, interrogations, the crowning with thorns, and the scourging exhausted him, even before his passion. Let me also be able to accept my cross and not be disheartened or discouraged by its difficulty.

People: O Jesus, teach me to hold your image on the cross in my hands and my heart, that I may have the wisdom to understand these words: "For whoever would save his life will lose it, but whoever loses his life for my sake will find it."

Our Father... Hail Mary... Glory Be...

℣. Lord Jesus, crucified,

℟. Have mercy on us!

> Through her heart, His sorrow sharing,
> All His bitter anguish bearing,
> Now at length, the sword has passed.

*But he was wounded for our transgressions,
he was bruised for our iniquities;*

Isaiah 53:5

Third Station

Jesus Falls the First Time

℣. We adore Thee, O Christ, and we praise Thee,

℟. Because by Thy holy cross Thou hast redeemed the world.

Leader: Jesus, because of the weight of the cross and the noise of the pushing crowd, you begin to feel weak, unstable and shaky. You start stumbling on the stony road, and suddenly you fall to the ground. Let me remember this as I struggle and fall in my pilgrimage of life.

People: O Lord, be my strength when I become discouraged. I cannot depart from you. I will arise again and go on. Once again, I will look at your saints and discover in them a hidden greatness.

Our Father... Hail Mary... Glory Be...

℣. Lord Jesus, crucified,

℟. Have mercy on us!

> O how sad and sore distressed
> Was that Mother, highly blest,
> Of the sole-begotten One!

When Jesus saw his mother and the disciple whom he loved standing near, he said to his mother, "Woman, behold, your son!" Then he said to the disciple, "Behold, your mother!"

John 19:26-27

Fourth Station

Jesus meets his Sorrowful Mother

℣. We adore Thee, O Christ, and we praise Thee,

℟. Because by Thy holy cross Thou hast redeemed the world.

Leader: For a short time, the eyes of Jesus and Mary, his Mother, met in a sorrow beyond description. It was just a brief moment, and yet it contained everything: their love, their pain, their determination and their obedience to the Will of the Eternal Father. Mary help me now to accept the call to holiness.

People: O Lady of Mercy! I am with you, I remember, and am determined to cherish the love of Jesus for me, the love that you have given me. May this love and devotion to your sweet name reign in my heart and engage all my emotions.

Our Father... Hail Mary... Glory Be...

℣. Lord Jesus, crucified,

℟. Have mercy on us!

> Christ above in torment hangs,
> She beneath beholds the pangs
> Of her dying glorious Son.

And they compelled a passerby, Simon of Cyrene, who was coming in from the country, the father of Alexander and Rufus, to carry his cross.

Mark 15:21

Fifth Station

Simon of Cyrene Helps Jesus to Carry His Cross

℣. We adore Thee, O Christ, and we praise Thee,

℟. Because by Thy holy cross Thou hast redeemed the world.

Leader: Simon, probably forced to carry the cross, did not realise who he was helping. The important thing was he actually helped. A kindhearted person would respond in the same way. Let us never forget those that struggle alongside us.

People: May we always have the courage and strength to ask for or accept the help offered by other people, but always arranged by Divine Providence! Let us always remember that what we do to the least of these, we do unto Jesus.

Our Father... Hail Mary... Glory Be...

℣. Lord Jesus, crucified,

℟. Have mercy on us!

> Is there one who would not weep,
> Whelmed in miseries so deep,
> Christ's dear Mother to behold?

"Truly, I say to you, as you did it to one of the least of these my brethren, you did it to me."

Matthew 25:40

Sixth Station

Veronica Wipes the Face of Jesus

℣. We adore Thee, O Christ, and we praise Thee,

℟. Because by Thy holy cross Thou hast redeemed the world.

Leader: Out of great compassion, a courageous woman by the name of Veronica wipes the bloody, sweaty face of her beloved Master on his way to Calvary. O St. Veronica, you have done what I would do when I look on the afflicted face of my beloved Redeemer. Help me to see Jesus in all the afflicted – a little kindness and, above all, a prayer can change sadness into joy.

People: O Jesus Christ, teach me to dry the tears, not only of my loved ones but also those that stream down the faces of all those Christ has asked me to call my family.

Our Father... Hail Mary... Glory Be...

℣. Lord Jesus, crucified,

℟. Have mercy on us!

> Can the human heart refrain
> From partaking in her pain,
> In that Mother's pain untold?

He was oppressed, and he was afflicted, yet he opened not his mouth; like a lamb that is led to the slaughter.

Isaiah 53:7

Seventh Station

Jesus falls the Second Time

℣. We adore Thee, O Christ, and we praise Thee,

℟. Because by Thy holy cross Thou hast redeemed the world.

Leader: What caused Jesus to fall again? Certainly not the cross. Simon of Cyrene carried it. Yes, Jesus noticed an evil desire in my soul beginning to take root. That is the real reason for the Saviour's fall. Jesus cautions me with the words, once addressed to St. Peter: "Simon, Simon, the devil has demanded your soul." I ask and then answer with St. Paul the Apostle: "I am a miserable man! Who will deliver me from the death of the flesh? The grace of God, through Jesus Christ."

People: O Lord, defend me from Satan's snares and the frailty of my will.

Our Father... Hail Mary... Glory Be...

℣. Lord Jesus, crucified,

℟. Have mercy on us!

> Bruised, derided, cursed, defiled,
> She beheld her tender child,
> All with bloody scourges rent.

But Jesus turning to them, said, "Daughters of Jerusalem, do not weep for me, but weep for yourselves and your children."

Matthew 23:27-28

Eighth Station

Jesus consoles the Women of Jerusalem

℣. We adore Thee, O Christ, and we praise Thee,

℟. Because by Thy holy cross Thou hast redeemed the world.

Leader: Often, the world feels sorry for those who scorn it to serve God and his people exclusively. In its eyes, they seem foolish and naïve for not developing and using their skills cunningly, but it is a false, pagan sympathy. Behold our Lord and God who teaches us in the light of eternity by saying: "Come, you blessed of my Father, inherit the kingdom, prepared for you from the very foundation of the world."

People: O Jesus, teach me to guard and increase the gift of my baptism's grace and be able to weep for all my many sins.

Our Father... Hail Mary... Glory Be...

℣. Lord Jesus, crucified,

℟. Have mercy on us!

> For the sins of His own nation
> Saw him hang in desolation
> Till His spirit forth He sent.

For we have not a high priest who is unable to sympathise with our weaknesses, but one who in every respect has been tempted as we are, yet without sinning.

Hebrews 4:15

Ninth Station

Jesus falls the Third Time

℣. We adore Thee, O Christ, and we praise Thee,

℟. Because by Thy holy cross Thou hast redeemed the world.

Leader: A great loss of physical strength caused Jesus to collapse again shortly before he arrived at the hill of Calvary. Before his public mission, Jesus was tempted by the devil upon another hill. O Lord, it was not the devil who struck you down. It was me. Through my arrogance and pride, I pushed and knocked you over.

People: O Holy Spirit, give me the gift of prudence and courage that I may always resist the lustful thoughts and actions that tarnish purity of heart. O Immaculate Virgin Mary, my Mother, cover me with your mantle of purity.

Our Father... Hail Mary... Glory Be...

℣. Lord Jesus, crucified,

℟. Have mercy on us!

> O thou Mother! fount of love,
> Touch my spirit from above,
> Make my heart with thine accord.

And they crucified him, and divided his garments among them, casting lots for them, to decide what each should take.

Mark 15:24

Tenth Station

Jesus is Stripped of His Garments

℣. We adore Thee, O Christ, and we praise Thee,

℟. Because by Thy holy cross Thou hast redeemed the world.

Leader: The world, in its immoderate appetite for sensuality, goes so far as it dares to disrobe even the God-Man himself of his divine and human dignity. May the darkness of which the Gospels speak envelop the hill of Golgotha and cover the humiliated Lord, exposed to the jeer of the crowd. Lord, never allow me to be stripped of the sanctifying grace of baptism and fall deep into sin.

People: O Jesus, my Lord! May I never depart from your Holy Will because of the lack of vigilance on my part. Strip me rather of my own will to fill me with yours.

Our Father... Hail Mary... Glory Be...

℣. Lord Jesus, crucified,

℟. Have mercy on us!

> Make me feel as thou hast felt;
> Make my soul to glow and melt
> With the love of Christ my Lord.

There they crucified him with two others, one on either side and Jesus between them.

John 19:18

Eleventh Station

Jesus is Nailed to the Cross

℣. We adore Thee, O Christ, and we praise Thee,

℟. Because by Thy holy cross Thou hast redeemed the world.

Leader: "When they arrived at Golgotha, they crucified him there." Jesus himself stretched out his arms and feet for the nailing. This was his decision to obey his Father in everything. Allow me also to be able to leave everything and attach myself to the cross for love of God.

People: O Lord Jesus! To you, I want to offer everything, and for you, I desire to live and die. Defend me, O Lord Jesus, from the temptation to come down from the cross.

Our Father... Hail Mary... Glory Be...

℣. Lord Jesus, crucified,

℟. Have mercy on us!

> Holy Mother, pierce me through,
> in my heart each wound renew
> of my Saviour crucified.

And Jesus uttered a loud cry, and breathed his last. And the curtain of the temple was torn in two, from top to bottom.

Mark 15:37-38

Twelfth Station

Jesus Dies on the Cross

℣. We adore Thee, O Christ, and we praise Thee,

℟. Because by Thy holy cross Thou hast redeemed the world.

Leader: When we were still in the slavery of sin, Jesus delivered himself to death on the cross for our sake. St. John, the beloved Apostle, testified to this love when he wrote: "Those who were his own, he loved them to the end."

People: O Lord Jesus, I confess my weakness. I know that without you, I can do nothing. Inflame my soul with the fire of your love that I may love you above all things and my brothers for your sake, remembering the words of St. Paul, the Apostle: "but without love, nothing can help me."

Our Father... Hail Mary... Glory Be...

℣. Lord Jesus, crucified,

℟. Have mercy on us!

> Let me share with thee His pain,
> Who for all my sins was slain,
> Who for me in torments died.

After this, Joseph of Arimathea ... took the body of Jesus and bound it in linen cloths with spices, as is the burial custom of the Jews.

John 19:38-40

Thirteenth Station

Jesus is Taken Down from the Cross

℣. We adore Thee, O Christ, and we praise Thee,

℟. Because by Thy holy cross Thou hast redeemed the world.

Leader: Mary, the Mother of all Sorrows, holds the dead body of her Son. With a broken heart, she cries out: "All of you, who pass by, see if there is any sorrow like my sorrow?" I earnestly desire, O Mother of all Sorrows, to place the moment of my death into your hands.

People: O my sweet Jesus, I will be eternally grateful to you in heaven that when on earth, I have followed your way, the simplest and the shortest, through Mary, our Mother. Give me the grace to always obey your Mother's request: "Do whatever he tells you."

Our Father... Hail Mary... Glory Be...

℣. Lord Jesus, crucified,

℟. Have mercy on us!

> Let me mingle tears with thee,
> Mourning Him Who mourned for me,
> All the days that I may live.

And he bought a linen shroud, and taking him down, wrapped him in the linen shroud, and laid him in a tomb which had been hewn out of the rock; and he rolled a stone against the door of the tomb.

Mark 15:46

Fourteenth Station

Jesus is Buried in the Tomb

℣. We adore Thee, O Christ, and we praise Thee,

℟. Because by Thy holy cross Thou hast redeemed the world.

Leader: The body of our beloved Redeemer, wrapped in the shroud, lies in peace in the niche hewn in the rock. Let me remember that there will be a last station on my earthly pilgrimage. When I am laid to rest, hear the prayer of those that pray for my soul: "Eternal rest grant unto them, O Lord, and let perpetual light shine upon them. May they rest in peace!"

People: O, my beloved Saviour, even now, I thank you for the grace I received at baptism and for the gift of the communion of saints. Be merciful to me on the day of my judgement!

Our Father... Hail Mary... Glory Be...

℣. Lord Jesus, crucified,

℟. Have mercy on us!

> By the Cross with thee to stay,
> There with thee to weep and pray,
> Ss all I ask of thee to give.

Now, the customary practice is to return to the altar and complete the devotion by saying the closing prayer.

Concluding Prayer

Though this journey of the *Way of the Cross* may now be complete, I must now go out and finish the pilgrimage of this life. May I always be able to hold the image of the cross before my eyes and be able to contemplate the price that was paid for my salvation. Remembering this price, may I be now filled with true contrition for all my sins and a desire to be ever more faithful to the grace I have been given.

One *Our Father*, *Hail Mary* and *Glory Be* is said for the intention of the Pope to gain the indulgences connected with the devotion of the *Stations of the Cross*.

Marian Valley

Marian Valley, the Shrine of Our Lady Help of Christians is situated at 2541 Beechmont Rd, 10km from Canungra and south of Brisbane in the Gold Coast Hinterland. As an Archdiocesan Shrine of Brisbane it is dedicated to Our Lady Help of Christians, a title under which Mary is particularly honoured in Australia as its Patroness.

At Marian Valley there are many beautiful chapels, donated by generous benefactors including different ethnic communities. The main Chapel is known as the Black Madonna Chapel. It houses a true copy of the Miraculous Icon of Our Lady of Czestochowa. There is a strong connection between the Pauline Fathers who are custodians of Marian Valley and the Blank Madonna, since they have also been custodians of the original Black Madonna icon for centuries.

One of the most beautiful and inspiring aspects of Marian Valley are the outdoor Stations of the Cross with their lifesize figures that move you to humility, devotion and prayer. Which are depicted in this book and are the inspiration for it.

Order of St. Paul The First Hermit

The Pauline Fathers and Brothers are more properly called the Order of St Paul the First Hermit (Ordo Sancti Pauli Primae Eremitae OSPPE). It is a Catholic Religious order of men. It is a Monastic order founded in the 13th century in Hungry. Its founders were hermits who came together to form a monastery and a religious community. Blessed Eusebius of Esztergom can be said to be the founder of this order. These Hermits chose St Paul the First Hermit to be their heavenly patron. In 1308 the Order official adopted the Rule of St Augustine.

The Pauline Fathers are dedicated to spreading devotion to Our Lady, particularly under the form of devotion to Our Lady of Czestochowa, the Black Madonna of which they have been custodians for centuries. The Pauline Fathers, who arrived in Australia in 1982, have two shrines devoted to her: The Shrine of Our Lady of Mercy and the Shrine of Our Lady Help of Christians.

www.ingramcontent.com/pod-product-compliance
Lightning Source LLC
Chambersburg PA
CBHW041500010526
44107CB00044B/1522